REI Editions

All our ebooks can be read on the following devices:

- Computer
- eReader
- iOS
- Android
- Blackberry
- Window
- Tablet
- Mobile phone

Mantelli - Brown - Kittel - Graf

Aggregate A4 - The V-2

ISBN: 9782372973366

Publication: January 2025

www.rei-editions.com

Mantelli - Brown - Kittel - Graf

Aggregate A4
The V-2

REI Editions

Index

The V- 2

The V-2 missile was the precursor to ballistic missiles and was used extensively by Germany during the later stages of World War II, particularly against Great Britain and Belgium.

- The acronym V-2 stands for Vergeltungswaffe 2, (retaliatory weapon 2 in German, an idea of Joseph Goebbels for propaganda purposes).

The missile was designated by its designers as A4 (Aggregat 4): as early as 1927, members of the German Society began the first tests on liquid-fueled rockets.
In 1932, the Reichswehr (German National Defense) became interested in the development of these tests especially for the military sector, and a team led by General Walter Dornberger was very impressed by the test of a carrier designed and built by Wernher von Braun.
Although the characteristics of this first rocket were very limited, Dornberger was able to sense von Braun's genius and, therefore, encouraged him to join the army in order to continue the development of his research: Von Braun accepted, as did many other members of the society.

- The A-4/V-2 missile was uninterceptable.
- A weapon against which there was no defense.

To date, only a deployment of Patriots or SA-10s could parry an attack, and at enormous cost, against what was an ancestor of the current Scuds, similar in performance and warhead but more precise and half the weight.
On September 6, 1944, when the V-1 missiles were already beginning to wane, V-2s began to be launched against Paris, but without success: on September 8, however, they began to strike London.

- Their arrival was without warning signs, no alarms or hisses.

The government pretended that it was a gas leak, but soon had to admit the threat: people did not take it too badly, since it was more fatalistic to see a building explode every now and then than to suffer the terror of sirens and anti-aircraft guns, and clusters of bombs falling from the sky.
The Londoners continued to hope for victory and resisted, even though they suffered thousands of casualties.

- The only weapon sighted in the air by a Spitfire, which turned and attacked it, had disappeared into the clouds in no time.

Launching the V-2, however, was not easy: there were over 100 tons to carry around to launch such weapons; they had to be erected after having mounted the warhead, which contained Amatol, a low-power explosive but stable since upon re-entry into the atmosphere more powerful explosives would have exploded, as often happened, despite the thick fiberglass structure used for insulation.

- The next stage was to erect the weapon with the warhead on a reusable metal platform (up to a dozen times), and then refuel the device with 4,173 kg of ethyl alcohol and 5,533 kg of oxygen.

It was difficult, almost as if it were an experimental program, rather than an operational weapon, and it was dangerous if there were problems, for example, if there was a strong crosswind.
Preparing for the V-2 launch was difficult, requiring 28-30 support vehicles.

A whole other world compared to the single, high-mobility truck of the evolved descendants of the Scud missiles.

The missile was ready after hours of work and it was also necessary to be careful of air raids, with the Typhoons always flying around at low altitude, since the range of the V-2s was limited and could not be increased much.

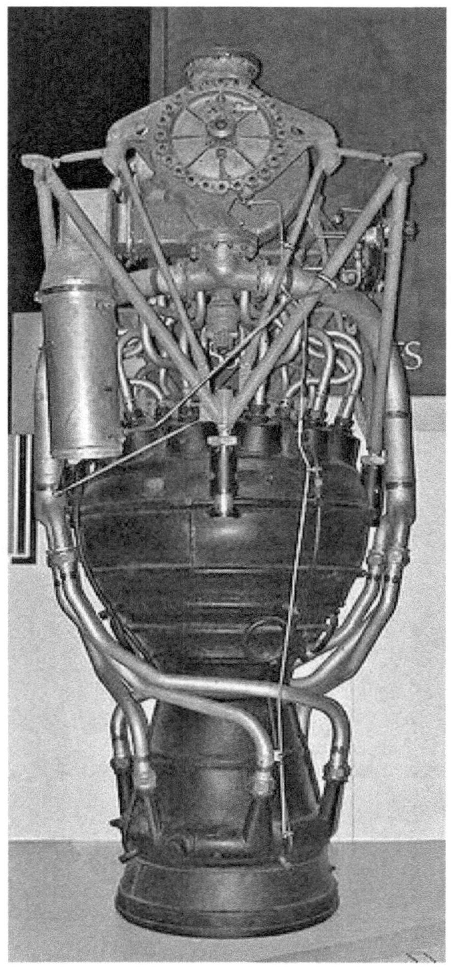

The A4 rocket engine with turbopump, gas generator and thrust structure.

- The weapon was not very accurate, about 4 km from the center of the target, but it was a little better, nevertheless, than the V-1.

The latter was interceptable, but, after all, it carried, roughly, the same charge over the same distances, but at a much lower weight and cost, as well as with a system that was easier to produce and use.

Some of the V-2's remarkable engineering can be seen in this sectional view of the turbine fuel pump. It ran at 5,000 rpm and was powered by steam generated by two auxiliary fuels.
Deutsches Technikmuseum in Berlin.

Later, V-2s were also conceived that could be launched from special containers towed by submarines, and even V-2s with wings, an ingenious but difficult to implement system to better exploit the weapon's energy.
In short, the potential of the endoreactor, powered by a 730 hp

turbopump that mixed the components in the combustion chamber, while the jet was diverted with graphite panels according to the internal stabilized platform which was the guidance system, was exploited for a long time: even the colossal Soviet rockets of the R-7 Semyorka type were still based on that type of endoreactor, with 20 engines mounted in parallel to form a more powerful one.

- And, despite the complication, this complex used by the Soviets has proven to function with remarkable reliability.

Related to the V-2 was the Rocket U-boat, a secret German military project to create the first ballistic missile submarine capable of launching SLBMs (Submarine-launched ballistic missiles).

The idea, later abandoned, was conceived by the Third Reich during the Second World War: the original plan envisaged the use of German U-boats for an attack on New York City using the new V2 missiles.

- In 1941, the idea was to adapt the U-511 unit of the Type IX-C U-boat class, which had already confirmed the validity of the idea from the first experiments, being able to release missiles from its upper part, both when surfaced and when submerged up to a depth of 12 metres.

However, at that time, Germany was more focused on the development of the V-1, and thus, this project was put aside.

In 1943 the project was revived after the V-1 had reached the operational stage: once again, however, the plan to use the V-1 on a U-boat was shelved.

- This project was discussed again in 1943-44 in a more advanced form, with the planning of the attack on New York: code name Prufstand XII.

For this mission, it was intended to use V-2 missiles, but the submarines were not capable of carrying them, and so it was decided to move on to another solution: to mount the V-2 inside a large, watertight cylindrical container that would be towed across the Atlantic: after reaching its launch position, the V-2 would be launched at New York.
To this end, it was thought to use the Type XXI U-boat, which would have towed three containers across the Atlantic, containers which, in addition to the V-2, would also have contained the fuel reserve (diesel fuel) intended to power the submarine during its voyage.

- To launch the missile, the ballast tanks in the container would be flooded, bringing it into a vertical position to be launched toward its target.

However, the Allies were aware of Germany's missile program and had drawn up a contingency plan, codenamed Operation Teardrop, which consisted of using four carrier battle groups to prevent U-boats from penetrating the American coast.
And, indeed, in March 1945, a group of six Type IX-C U-boats were intercepted off the American coast and four submarines were sunk, although it was later established that this was not a V-2 missile attack.

- Between September 1944 and February 1945, a total of 5,300 V-2s were manufactured at Mittelwerk.

2,800 were dropped, of which about half hit their target: 1,050 fell on England, killing 2,754 people and injuring 6,523, destroying 400,000 homes, as well as damaging 4,000,000 others.
Belgium suffered the same fate.

In October 1944, London was hit by 25 V-2s and Antwerp by 10; the deadliest launch occurred over Antwerp on 16 December

1944: 561 people were killed in a cinema.

History

As early as 1929, the German military invested in research into the military use of rockets.

The aim was, in particular, to find a way to circumvent the restrictions of the Treaty of Versailles which limited the development of the German air force.

The person responsible for this research was Karl Becker, a career soldier and artillery engineer, whose completion he entrusted to Captain Walter Dornberger: he was responsible for the development of solid-propellant rockets weighing between 5 and 9 kg and for carrying out theoretical research on liquid-propellant propulsion.

A firing range located in Kummersdorf, on the outskirts of Berlin, was used between 1930 and 1932 to launch solid-fuel rockets.

The Air Force, for which von Braun developed the take-off assist rockets, as well as the Army, on which Dornberger and Becker depended, were prepared to make significant financial resources available.

By 1936, von Braun's team had grown to 80 people and the Kummersdorf camp had become too small for the planned tests: at the suggestion of von Braun's mother, the facilities were moved to Peenemünde, a location 250 km north of Berlin on the island of Usedom, along the Baltic Sea coast.

The chosen site, in the north of the island, is difficult to access and uninhabited, and meets the specifications of a secret project, while the islet of Greifswalder Oie, located about ten kilometers offshore, constitutes an ideal launch zone.

The German Air Force and Army are funding 11 million marks for a complex of housing, industrial facilities and testing equipment that will house more than 2,000 scientists and engineers, as well as more than 4,000 technicians and workers.

Two facilities are being built next to each other: the western part with an area of 10 km 2 is occupied by the Air Force, which has a landing field for experimental aircraft, but with modest facilities because no research activities are planned on site.

The eastern part, where researchers and technicians led by von Braun were installed in May 1937, included a plant for the production of liquid oxygen, a small port and a series of rather luxurious accommodations for the new arrivals.

The main technical buildings and test benches are located at the northern end of the island.

The increased power required by the 25 tons of thrust of the A4 engine required a complete overhaul of the rocket engine design.

Thiel, a particularly gifted and imaginative doctor of chemistry, made four decisive discoveries:

- It gives the injector nozzle holes a shape that imparts a rotary motion to the liquid oxygen droplets, thus homogenizing the mixture and increasing the expulsion speed of the burnt gases from 1,700 to 1,900 m/s.
- It places the injectors in a pre-chamber at the top of the combustion chamber, further improving the mixing process.
- It shortens the combustion chamber by increasing its diameter: the reduction in volume allows for an increase in efficiency and a reduction in weight.
- Optimize the shape of the nozzle. The angle with the vertical had until then been fixed at 10-12°, but the experiments carried out by Thiel allowed him to demonstrate that an angle of 30°, reducing the frictional forces between the burned gases and the nozzle wall, allowed to reach the expected expulsion velocity of 2,000 m/s.

After trying several configurations that resulted in burning or

cooling problems, Thiel settled on a configuration with 18 mushroom-shaped injectors.
To cool the walls of the combustion chamber brought to the temperature of 2,400° C, Thiel's team came up with fluid film cooling, which consists of circulating along the internal wall of the combustion chamber a fluid that is colder than the combustion gases, thus preventing the structure from reaching its melting point.

- Four rows of holes placed at different heights of the combustion chamber inject a film of ethanol (ethyl alcohol) which dissipates 90% of the total heat.

Ethanol circulating in a double wall at the top of the combustion chamber absorbs the remaining heat through regenerative cooling.
The jet deflectors, located at the nozzle exit, have the task of correcting the trajectory during the propulsion phase but are subject to very high temperatures: in fact, the tungsten and molybdenum alloys, initially tested, proved unsatisfactory and were replaced by carbon.

- The engine is fed with propellant via a turbopump to reach the necessary pressure in the combustion chamber.

The first studies were inspired by the fire pumps developed by the Klein, Schanzlin and Becker company: however, the adaptation of these models to the extreme temperatures generated by liquid oxygen, and the mass constraint, required solutions that reached the limits of the technical knowledge of the time.
To drive the turbopump von Braun chose a gas generator (water vapor) using hydrogen peroxide , developed by Hellmuth Walter for the second experimental version of a Heinkel He 112, to which a rocket engine, the He 112R, was added. The development of the entire propulsion system was only

completed in 1941.

Development of the V-2 began around May 1937, but there was no initial test of the propulsion on a testbed until 21 March 1940.

The first complete rocket was taken to the test stand for a static test in October 1940, but the launch was postponed throughout the first half of 1941 because numerous problems arose: poor quality welds, problems in the management of the valves and controls of the rocket motor, development of the injection system piping and of the turbopump/gas generator unit.

Static tests were completed only in the summer of 1941, and the rocket engine was first fired on the test stand in September 1941.

- However, the problems are far from being solved.

An early V-2 explodes on the launch pad, severely damaging it, while a rocket engine explodes on the engine test stand on November 5.

Domberger strongly criticizes the engineers in charge of the center (Wehrner von Braun, Thiel and Riedel) for having let inexperienced engineers take care of these tests for them and for having wasted too much time on production preparations.

The first flight finally took place on June 13, 1942.

The missile takes off and then disappears behind the very low cloud ceiling: it breaks the sound barrier but the propulsion stops following the exhaustion of the electric battery, resulting from the very rapid rolling movement that began at the moment of launch.

The V-2 eventually crashed into the sea about 600 meters from the shore. The second flight took place on August 16, 1942.

The rocket takes off this time without rolling and exceeds the speed of Mach 2 but the propulsion stops 45 seconds after liftoff, instead of the planned 60 seconds, and it crashes just 8.7 kilometers from the launch site.

After several modifications, in particular the strengthening of the rocket nose, a third launch took place on 3 October 1942 and was a total success.

- The rocket rose to an altitude of 80 kilometers and crashed into the sea 190 kilometers from the starting point.

In December 1942, Albert Speer managed to convince a reluctant Hitler to begin mass production of A4s for use as weapons: given the Allied air threat, it was proposed to launch the V-2s towards the south of the United Kingdom, from pillboxes set up along the French coast.
The technicians of Peenemünde had designed these enormous plants which would have allowed:

- House the fuel and oxidizer under several feet of concrete.
- Technical rooms for the production of liquid oxygen and the execution of tests, as well as warehouses for missiles.
- A transport system for missiles.
- The barracks housed 250 to 300 specialists, all protected by anti-aircraft batteries.

Domberger, however, had a completely different idea: for him only mobile squads, consisting of soldiers who had received specialized training, could evade the Allied fighters. In the end, German officials decided to create a pillbox battery and two mobile batteries.
Work on the battery under the fort was entrusted to the Todt organisation and began in March 1943 at Eperlecques near Calais.
The site was chosen because it was within range of the regions hit by the missiles, close to a railway line and relatively sheltered from air attacks by both terrain and vegetation.
The Eperlecques blockhouse, a gigantic structure, quickly

employed several thousand people, mainly Frenchmen mobilised by the STO (Compulsory Labour Service, which provided, during the occupation of France by Germany, for the requisition and transfer to Germany of hundreds of thousands of French workers against their will, to participate in the German war effort) because 120,000 m3 of concrete was to be poured.
Already in May, however, the photos taken by reconnaissance planes had alerted the Allies: although they did not know the purpose of the installation, they decided to launch a massive bombing.

- On August 27, 366 one-ton bombs were dropped on the site, causing damage that led to the Germans abandoning the site.

Following the bombing of Eperlecques, German leaders decided to build the armored battery in a former gypsum quarry located not far away in the commune of Helfaut, near Saint-Omer. The installation included an immense concrete dome (the Helfaut dome) 71 meters in diameter and 5 meters thick, under which a network of tunnels and rooms was to be dug. The construction site was, in turn, regularly bombed in March 1944, but without significant results.
However, on July 17, 1944, a raid using giant Tallboy bombs shook the ground enough to destabilize the foundations of the otherwise intact dome.
The Germans therefore decided to definitively abandon the idea of building launching stations sheltered in pillboxes, and to entrust the launching to mobile launch battalions.
Following the abandonment of the armored pillboxes, specialized units were formed to launch the missiles.

A V2 rocket at the Peenemünde museum.

The chosen organization aimed to simplify the launch operations as much as possible to reduce preparation times and allow the use of unprepared sites.

- The V-2 missiles were delivered by rail and then stored in workshops located a few kilometers from the launch sites:

teams of technicians assigned to the workshop checked the functioning of the missiles before delivering them to the launch teams who, once the launch site had been chosen, loaded the propellants before carrying out the launch itself.

SS General Hans Kammler, who directed V-2 production, created two V-2 launch units during the summer of 1944, each consisting of more than 5,000 men and approximately 1,600 specialized vehicles: eight battalions each consisting of three launch units.

The Northern Group, based near Nijmegen, Netherlands, comprised the battalions 1./485, 2./485, 3./485.

The southern grouping, formed at the beginning of the campaign around Euskirchen, Germany, included the battalions 1./836, 2./836, 3./836, 1./444, 2./444 and 3./444 16.

- The first V-2 was launched on 8 September 1944 from Gouvy, Belgium, heading towards Paris.

In 5 minutes it reached Maisons-Alfort, a suburb of Paris, causing 6 deaths and 36 injuries: "Paris had just had the formidable privilege of being the first target of a military ballistic device".

On the same day, Duncan Sandys, chairman of the British Flying Bomb Committee, declared at a press conference that "apart from a few possible final blows," the battle for London was complete.

The first V-2 launched against London fell at Chiswick: it would take two months and 200 explosions on English soil before the British government announced the V-2 attacks.

The secret was all the easier to keep because , unlike the V-1s which had a characteristic hum reminiscent of a motorcycle engine, the missiles reached a speed of Mach 3.5, greater than the speed of sound, that is, in total silence, therefore, the

explosions could be attributed to any type of cause.
And, in fact, when the first V-2 fell on London, no one at the time realised that it was a bomb: it was believed that a building had exploded because of the gas, until the debris of the missile was discovered.

- In all, 4,000 V-2s were built to be launched towards London and the United Kingdom.

Entering service very late, the V-2s were launched from sites that the advance of the Allied troops required to be moved several times: in the Netherlands from the Middelburg region and especially The Hague, allowing them to reach London, then from Rijs, the Norfolk region, Hellendoorn and Dalfsen, towards Belgium and the bridge at Remagen.
In Belgium and the Rhineland, the launches took place from Saint-Vith and Mertzig towards Paris, then from the surroundings of Koblenz towards northern France and Belgium.
The last batteries were installed in the Münster region, with Antwerp and Liège as their destination.

- Despite the damage inflicted on production and launch facilities, 1,560 V-2s were launched between September 8 and the end of 1944.

The launch of another 1,500 V-2s continued until 27 March 1945, mainly from The Hague, and always towards London, the main civilian target of the Germans, and Antwerp, as well as towards some military targets: the last rockets were launched towards Kent.

- The launch units had around thirty specialized vehicles to enable the launch.

The V-2 missiles manufactured at Mittelwerk were delivered by rail to the nearest station, transported on specialized trailers, the Vidalwagen, and then stored in workshops located a few kilometers from the launch sites.

- Each workshop could store about 30 missiles but, where possible, storage time was limited to a few days, because during testing it had been noted that the fragile rocket components degraded rapidly over time.

In these laboratories, teams of workshop technicians checked the functioning of the missiles, set the explosive charge, then transported each V-2 using a Vidalwagen close to the firing site, to an improvised location, if possible sheltered from enemy reconnaissance aircraft.

There, the missile was transferred to the firing unit's Meillerwagen erector vehicle using a removable gantry developed for handling tank turrets.

It was then cared for by the launch team who, after choosing a launch site, installed it on a circular launch pad with four supports under the missile's fins.

- In the center of the launch pad was a cone of thick steel plate to deflect the jet of burning gases.

The launch platform could be positioned on any flat, stable terrain (portion of road, small concrete area), or even on a simple platform made of railway sleepers embedded in well-compacted soil, which therefore allowed the missile to be deployed practically anywhere.

The launch team loaded the propellants before carrying out the launch: this last phase took place in just under 2 hours.

The liquid oxygen was transported in a tanker truck that loaded it at a permanent station: since oxygen remains liquid only at a temperature of -183° C, much of it evaporated during transport.

- The tanker therefore carried 6,400 kg while the missile only needed 4,900 kg.

For the launch, the power increase of the propulsion system

occurred in two stages.
At ignition, the initial thrust was 3 tons, which did not allow the missile to take off, but gave technicians time to visually check the flame produced, thus ensuring that the engine was working properly.
After 3 seconds, the thrust increased to 25 tons and the V-2 took off.
The rocket engine ran for 65-70 seconds.

- Acceleration gradually increased and reached 8g, when the engine cut out at an altitude of 35 km.

At the end of its powered flight, the V-2 continued on a purely ballistic trajectory like a grenade.

- Due to inertia, the missile continued on an ascending trajectory that reached a peak of 97 km, before starting to lose altitude, crashing into the ground at a speed of between 3,200 and 3,600 km/h.

Flying at a speed greater than the speed of sound, it struck without first being heard.
When the V-2 was launched at a target located at a distance close to its maximum range, its trajectory was relatively imprecise: in fact, the distance between the target and the area actually hit was between 7 and 17 km, which made the weapon unusable for military purposes.
Towards the end of the war the Germans used a radio guidance system, the Leitstrahlstellung, which improved this accuracy , but its use was limited to the SS 500 battery stationed near Dalfsen/Hellendoorn in the Netherlands.
Despite its innovative nature as an air-to-air missile, the V-2's impact was primarily psychological.

- Compared to conventional bombing, these early ballistic missiles, imprecise, manufactured in relatively limited numbers and carrying a small explosive charge, played only a marginal role at the strategic or tactical level.

A single conventional heavy bomber cost much less for much greater destructive capacity and accuracy, and was reusable.

- But the V-2 paved the way for modern weapons that became the mainstay of nuclear deterrence and so-called "surgical" strikes in the last third of the 20th century.

The V-2, in fact, was a practically unstoppable weapon, unlike the V-1, but it required long and complex manufacturing for a charge of less than a ton of explosive and poor precision.

- No notable military or industrial targets were hit by the V-2.

Its role was above all propagandistic, to maintain the illusions of the Führer and of German public opinion, convinced that secret weapons would change the fate of the war.
A tactical failure, but, nevertheless, a brilliant technical success: the V-2, in fact, is directly at the origin of intercontinental missiles, but also of space flight and the conquest of space.
The V-2 missile played a decisive role in the post-war period in the development of ballistic missiles and then of launchers at the end of the 1950s, because it allowed the development of numerous techniques that are still often used today:

- It was, by far, the most powerful missile built at the time, and thus contributed decisively to the creation of high-thrust missile engines.
- The V-2 used for the first time a turbopump powered by a gas generator to supply the propellant.
- It was the first missile to have an engine whose thrust could be modulated, at the end of the propulsion phase, to 31% of the nominal phase.
- It was the first missile to have an autonomous guidance system, capable of correcting its trajectory by taking into

account movements in the atmosphere.

Aware of the immense progress made by German engineers and technicians, the Allies therefore did everything they could to exploit the equipment, documentation and specialists.
And, in fact, the United States, during Operation Paperclip, exfiltrated and recruited important German rocket scientists including Wernher von Braun, Walter Dornberger, Adolf Thiel, Hermann Oberth and Arthur Rudolph.

- They recovered more than 100 V-2s in the Mittelwerk factory, which they were the first to occupy, before ceding this part of the territory to the Soviets.

The V-2s were transported to the United States for study and then launched from the White Sands launch center in New Mexico beginning in 1946.
The V-2s were also the first sounding rockets capable of reaching more than 100 km and of studying the upper atmosphere using on-board scientific instruments.

- On October 24, 1946, a V-2 was used to take the first photograph of the Earth from space at an altitude of 105 km, using a 35 mm Devry motion picture camera attached to the missile.

Additionally, several missiles were developed directly from the V-2, such as the Bumper, a modified V-2 topped by an American WAC Corporal rocket, including the first two launches from Cape Canaveral in July 1950.

- The Viking missile is an improved copy of the V-2 missile, half the size, which was used as a sounding rocket between 1949 and 1955 and then served as the first stage for the lightweight Vanguard launcher, developed to place America's first artificial satellite into orbit.

The German specialists repatriated to the United States were later transferred to Fort Bliss, Texas, an Army facility responsible for ballistic missile development.
In 1950, von Braun was appointed technical director of the U.S. Army's Redstone Arsenal facility located in Huntsville, Alabama, dedicated to the development of guided missiles.
His team of German engineers developed the Redstone air-to-air missile, directly derived from the German V-2, and the U.S. military's first guided ballistic missile, which would be used in 1961 to launch the first American astronauts.

- In 1956, von Braun was appointed director of research for the U.S. Army Ballistic Missile Agency, where his team oversaw the development of the Pershing and Jupiter missiles.

The first American satellite, Explorer 1, was launched by a Juno I rocket designed primarily by German engineers.
The V-2 was , however, a resounding success in scientific terms, as it reached a much greater apogee than Von Braun had predicted, passing beyond the mesosphere and reaching the thermosphere, the penultimate layer of the Earth's atmosphere.

Technical features

The V-2 missile was a 12.5-ton machine (4.5 tons empty) powered by a rocket engine burning a mixture of ethanol and liquid oxygen and exerting a take-off thrust of 25 tons.

- It took off from a launch pad that could be moved and was accelerated for 65 seconds to a speed of 1,341 km/s (4,827 km/h).

It had a gyroscopic guidance system that adapted the trajectory by means of control surfaces located on the empennage and jet deflectors located at the nozzle exit.
Its trajectory reached a peak of about 90 km and it carried a military charge consisting of 750 kilograms of explosives up to a distance of 320 km.
The missile was propelled for more than 60 seconds by a rocket engine burning a fuel composed of 75% ethanol and 25% water, called B-Stoff, with oxygen stored in liquid form at a temperature of -183° C.
The pressure in the combustion chamber was 15 bar and the propellants had to be injected into it under higher pressure.

- A turbopump rotating at 3,800 rpm was responsible for increasing the pressure of the fuel coming from the tank to 23 bar and that of the oxygen to 17.5 bar.

Its 580 hp turbine was powered by water vapor produced by a gas generator using a mixture of sodium permanganate and hydrogen peroxide.
The combustion chamber, whose temperature reached 2,500° C, was cooled in various ways so that its walls did not melt.

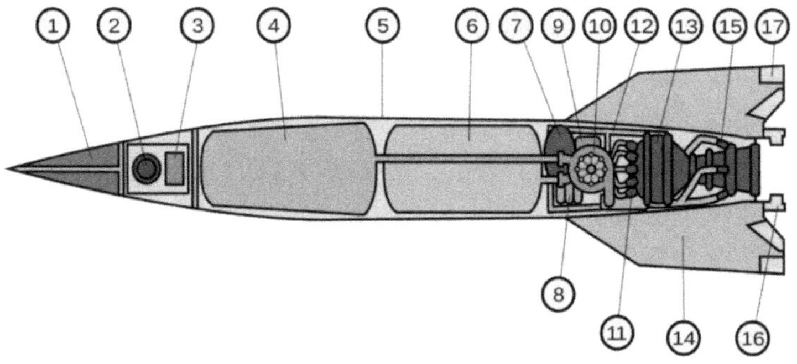

1. Explosive charge
2. Gyroscopic system
3. Guide and radio control
4. Ethanol tank
5. Fuselage
6. Liquid oxygen tank
7. Hydrogen peroxide tank
8. Pressurized nitrogen cylinder
9. Hydrogen peroxide reaction chamber
10. Turbo pump
11. Ethanol/Oxygen Injectors
12. Engine frame
13. Combustion chamber
14. Tail (x4)
15. Nozzle
16. Graphite Jet Deflectors (x4)
17. External rudders (x4)

From a technical point of view, it was a liquid-fueled rocket , weighing 13,500 kg at launch, with:

- Height: 14 meters.
- Diameter: 1.65 meters.
- Engine: 730 hp power, 26,000 kgs thrust at sea level.
- Guidance system: radio
- Explosive load: approximately 1 ton of Amatol or Nippolit.
- Range: between 320 and 360 kilometers.
- Maximum speed: 5,760 km/h.
- Empty weight: 4 tons.
- Takeoff weight: 12 tons.
- Fuel weight:
  - ❖ Liquid oxygen: 4,910 kg
  - ❖ Ethanol: 2.857 kg (75%)
  - ❖ Water: 953 kg (25%)
- Weight of turbo pump fluids:
  - ❖ 0.0076 tons of potassium permanganate.
  - ❖ 0.175 tons of hydrogen peroxide.
  - ❖ The mixture of these two liquids produced a vapor that mixed in the combustion chamber with the liquid oxygen and alcohol sent under pressure.
- Explosive: TNT and ammonium nitrate for a total of 1,000 kg (Amatol)
- Specimens: 5,200:
  - ❖ Up to September 15, 1944: 1,900
  - ❖ September 15 - October 29, 1944: 900
  - ❖ October 30 - November 24, 1944: 600
  - ❖ November 24 - January 15, 1945: 1,100
  - ❖ January 16 - February 15, 1945: 700

Upon explosion, the V-2 was capable of creating a crater 20 metres wide and 8 metres deep, ejecting approximately 3,000 tonnes of material into the air.

Aggregate

Aggregat is a family of rockets developed by German engineer Wernher von Braun and his team for Germany between 1933 and 1945.

Indicated by the letter A followed by a progressive number (from 1 to 12), they remained largely on paper.

- Particularly famous is the A4, which actually entered service under the name V-2.

More advanced versions included guided rockets and ballistic missiles capable of reaching the continental United States, but they were never built.

A1

The A1 rocket was the first of the Aggregat series.
It was designed in 1933 by Wernher von Braun as part of a Wehrmacht research program at Kummersdorf, under the guidance of Walter Dornberger.

- From a technical point of view, this rocket was 1.4 meters long, with a diameter of 0.3 meters.

The launch weight was 150 kg, of which 40 kg were propellant, a mixture of liquid oxygen and 75% alcohol.
From bottom to top the arrangement was as follows: the 300 kg thrust engine was mounted inside the fuel tank of 75% ethyl alcohol plus 25% water (the water was used to keep the combustion temperature low), while advances in the surface hardening of aluminium had allowed this metal to be used for the combustion chamber.

- Above this integral construction was the liquid oxygen tank, also made of aluminum, but with an internal fiberglass lining.

Then, on top, there was a sphere of compressed nitrogen to force both components of the propellant into the engine.
All three of these sections were enclosed within a robust cylinder which was airtight and allowed the pressurization to act equally on both the fuel and the oxidizer.

- The A-1's heaviest single component was a 70-pound nose-mounted gyroscopic flywheel that had to be spun at up to 9,000 rpm by an external electric motor.

This method of stabilization had been suggested by the Kummersdorf gunners, in parallel with ideas based on the rotation of projectiles when fired from cannons.

- The gyroscope would provide "brute force" stability as it rotated on the centerline axis and was fixed to the rocket structure.

The pressure engine designed by Rudolph was supposed to provide 300 kg of thrust for 16 seconds, however, the prototype exploded on the launch pad and the project was abandoned because it was considered unstable, and no launches were ever carried out.
As a result, the project was never followed up, but formed the basis of the more advanced A2.

A2

The A2 missile was the first flying testbed of the program that would later lead to the V-2.

In total, two were launched, both in 1934 (December 19 and 20), which were codenamed Max and Moritz, respectively, reaching altitudes of 2.2 km (1.4 mi) and 3.5 km (2.2 mi), respectively.

It was a rather small system, slightly longer than the A1: 1.61 metres long and 0.31 metres in diameter.

- However, unlike the A1, the A2's stabilizing gyroscopes were in the center of the rocket, between the alcohol and oxygen tanks, making it more stable.

The rocket weighed 72 kilograms (159 lb) empty, with a takeoff weight of 107 kilograms (236 lb), including 35 kg of propellant, the same mixture of ethanol and liquid oxygen as the A1.

From 1936, the group led by von Braun concentrated on building the successors to the A-2 rocket, the A-3 and the A-4.

A3

The A3 was the first large rocket built by von Braun and his team.
From a technical point of view, it was a system 6.74 meters long, with a diameter of 0.67 meters and a width of 0.93 meters.

- The launch weight was 740 kg and the engine was powered by the usual mixture of ethanol and liquid oxygen (LOX-alcohol), with an operating time of 45 seconds and a thrust of 1,500 kg.

Additionally, inside the liquid oxygen tanks, a tank containing liquid nitrogen had been mounted: this was electrically heated, thus producing gaseous nitrogen for pressurizing the propellant.

- This rocket was also equipped with a guidance system consisting of three gyroscopes and two accelerometers.

The equipment was completed by a small video camera placed on the nose of the missile.
Each missile carried recording instruments to measure surface heating by friction or atmospheric temperature and pressure during a parachute descent from a height of 20 km.
The A3, however, was a complete failure, as not even one of the four test launches, carried out between 4 and 11 December 1937, succeeded:

- The first A3 was launched and made a perfect liftoff, but at just 3 seconds, the parachute opened and dangled into the exhaust, being badly burned. This event also brought the rocket horizontal and the engine automatically shut down when it tipped too far at 6.3 seconds from where it turned and fell under the remains of the parachute. After about twenty seconds it crashed back onto the island just 300 meters from the launch site, exploding violently on impact.

- The second launch was again a good takeoff, but again the parachute opened at 3 seconds and dragged the rocket sideways for a near-exact repeat of the December 4 launch. It also crashed just 5 meters from the shore and exploded before reaching the sea.

- The parachute was removed for the third launch on 8 December and a signal flare was installed in its place. The wind was stronger than on previous attempts and the rocket veered rapidly, reaching only about 100 metres (330 ft). The control system was unable to correct for the crosswind, and again the engine automatically shut down and the missile crashed 2 km from the coast.

- The last attempt on December 11 was almost identical. Again the missile was fired into strong winds and, after takeoff, it curved into the wind, the engine stopped and the missile fell into the sea where the remaining propellants exploded. Again there was no parachute fitted to this test missile.

According to another source, an A3 would have achieved a range of 12.1 km and an altitude of 18 km.
As a result, what was supposed to be a scaled-down model of the definitive and more powerful A4, the future V-2, had to be completely redesigned.
After a series of unsuccessful launches, the A3 was, in fact, abandoned and redesigned as the A5.

A4

The A4 was the first liquid-fueled rocket to enter operational service. Better known as the V-2, approximately 6,000 were built, and formed the basis for the American, Soviet, and French rocket programs.

The first launch was made on 23 March 1942 at the Peenemünde site, with actual entry into service starting in 1944.

- The A4's first flight, in March 1942, saw it fly about a mile and crash into the water.
- The second missile reached an altitude of 11 kilometers before exploding.
- The third launch, on October 3, 1942, was crowned with complete success: the A-4 missile followed an almost perfect trajectory and crashed 193 km away from the launch platform, at an altitude of over 80 km.

From a technical point of view, it was a liquid-propellant rocket weighing 12,805 kg at launch, with:

- Length: 14 meters.
- Diameter: 1.65 meters.
- Engine: 730 hp power, 26,000 kgs thrust at sea level.
- Explosive load: approximately 1 ton of Amatol or Nippolit.
- Range: between 320 and 360 kilometers.
- Approximate speed: 5,000 km/h.
- Empty weight: 4 tons.
- Takeoff weight: 12 tons.
- Fuel weight:
  - ❖ Liquid oxygen: 4.7 tons
  - ❖ Alcohol: 2.7 tons.

- Weight of turbo pump fluids:
    - 0.0076 tons of potassium permanganate.
    - 0.175 tons of hydrogen peroxide.
    - The mixture of these two liquids produced a vapor that mixed in the combustion chamber with the liquid oxygen and alcohol sent under pressure.

In addition to the "classic" version, launchable from the ground, one was proposed for use as a submarine (abandoned due to technical problems in 1944), an anti-aircraft version (Wasserfall, actually launched) and one equipped with wings with increased range and the possibility of human piloting (A4b, two examples launched, without a crew).

A5

The A5 was a small-scale test model of the A4 rocket, which replaced the previous scale model, the A3, which had been unsuccessful.
It flew from 1938 to 1942 and played a key role in testing the aerodynamics and technology of the A4.
It had the same rocket engine as the A3, but had a new control system and its shape more closely resembled that of the A4.
Seventy of them were produced, of which 25 were without engines or with monopropellant rockets to test their aerodynamics by launching them from airplanes.

- The missile was equipped with a parachute system for descent and could float for up to two hours before sinking, allowing it to be recovered by ship.

Both non-propulsion variants and monopropellant variants were built for flight launch testing.
The A5 had a length of 5.825 meters, a diameter of 0.78 meters and a take-off weight of 900 kg.
Like the A3, it was fueled by alcohol and liquid oxygen as an oxidizer.
The first launch of the A5 took place in the summer of 1938 at Greifswalder Oie and the first successfully conducted guided flights took place in October 1939, with the aim of testing the control systems planned for the A4.
The A5 reached its maximum altitude of 12 km.

A6

The A6 was the designation von Braun's men gave to the project of a piloted photographic reconnaissance missile that was, due to its performance characteristics, practically invulnerable.

- From a technical point of view, the study, carried out in 1943, was based on a version of the A5 test bench with a propulsion system consisting of a ramjet.

In detail, the project envisaged a 15.75-meter-long, 6.33-meter-diameter, human-piloted rocket that was to be launched vertically.

After launch, it was planned to reach a maximum altitude of 95 km, with reentry into the atmosphere at a supersonic glide speed.

Subsequently, the ignition of the engine, the aforementioned

ramjet, would have taken place, which would have had to maintain a speed of 2,900 km/h for 15-20 minutes: for the landing, the use of a parachute was planned, or a normal airport.
In Germany, this project was presented to the German Air Ministry, which however, having no need for such an aircraft, rejected it.
The ramjet is a jet engine and, conceptually, the simplest exojet.

- The ramjet reduces the complexity of the simple turbojet by eliminating the compressor and, consequently, the turbine that has to drive it, thanks to the speed of the aircraft itself which compresses the air entering the air intake.

As a consequence, the ramjet is unable to operate at a fixed point (i.e. stationary with respect to the air) and has poor performance at low speeds, due to the low compression ratio obtained from the air intake.
In the post-war period, however, both the United States and the Soviet Union used a similar, albeit unmanned, configuration in the construction of the SM-64 Navaho and Burya ramjet cruise missiles.

- The operating principle of the ramjet is the same as that of a traditional jet engine.

Outside air enters a dynamic intake, or air intake, and is compressed and mixed with fuel, before passing into the combustion chamber and being expelled out the rear through an exhaust nozzle, at a higher velocity than the inlet velocity.
When air enters this type of jet engine, even if the aircraft is traveling at supersonic speed, it is slowed down to subsonic speed due to the particular geometry of the ducts, shaped to generate a system of oblique impacts.
As the flow passes through these sectors of the engine, the velocity of the flow decreases, usually down to Mach 0.3, while

the pressure increases, thus producing, according to Bernoulli's principle, the so-called dynamic compression.
At high speeds this process can be very efficient and can compress enough air, and therefore enough oxygen (oxidizer or comburent), to allow effective combustion in the engine.

A7

The A7 was intended to be a scaled-down technology demonstrator of the A9 rocket, however, it was never built, and work was stopped in 1940.
However, it was supposed to be a rocket 5.91 meters long, with a diameter of 0.38 meters and a weight of 1,000 kg, with a take-off thrust of 15 kN.

The A7 missile was similar in structure to the A5, but had larger tail fins, 1,621 m^2, to achieve greater glide range. Two unpowered models of the A7 were dropped from aircraft to test flight stability, but powered tests were never carried out.

A8

The A8 was a project for a stretched version of the V-2, which would have used storable propellants, probably nitric acid and kerosene.
This system was developed in 1941, but construction of a prototype or demonstrator was never started.

However, in the post-war period, studies continued by the French, relating to the so-called Super V-2: it was an IRBM (intermediate-range ballistic missile, covering a range of 3,000-5,500 km), later cancelled because it was too ambitious, but which constituted the basis for the Veronique and Diamant missiles and, distantly, for the Ariane space launcher.

A9

The A9 was a rocket-powered aircraft project that was advanced in 1944. It was essentially a manned, winged version of the V-2, but its development was banned by the high command.

Despite this, however, von Braun continued to work on this project, which received the internal code name of A4b. Two examples of this aircraft flew.

According to the designers' intentions, this system would have had a launch weight of 16,259 kg, including 1,000 kg of payload, with a length of 14.18 meters and a diameter of 3.2 meters, and would have been able to transport its load 600 km away 17 minutes after launch.

Another variant of the A9, unmanned, was developed for use as a second stage on the A10 ballistic missile.

A10

The A10 was a two-stage intercontinental ballistic missile project with an estimated range of 5,000 km.
Development of this weapon system began in 1940, with a first flight planned for 1946.
The project, however, was blocked by superior orders in 1943, when it was decided to concentrate all efforts on the V-2. Von Braun, however, continued to work on the missile, in particular on the second stage (A9), which was tested under the designation of A4b.
It was not until late 1944 that Von Braun and his team were officially authorized to resume research on this strategic weapons system, which was codenamed Projekt Amerika (Project America).
However, this long-range weapon saw no practical development: the only real tests involved two flights of the A4b, the last of which in January 1945.

- According to the designers, the A10 was supposed to be a two-stage missile with liquid propellant (LOX and alcohol), the missile was supposed to have an overall height of 41 meters, with a diameter of 4.12 meters and a launch weight of 85,300 kg (of which 1,000 kg of war load): the range, as previously mentioned, was supposed to reach 5,000 km.

The missile's name was essentially due to the name of its two stages, which were called, precisely, A9 and A10. During the development phase, various configurations of these two stages were hypothesized.

- A10: This was the first stage of the missile.
  In its initial version, it was supposed to have an engine

consisting of a cluster of 6 A4 combustion chambers, liquid-fueled (LOX/alcohol), with a single exhaust nozzle.
Subsequently, it was decided to use an engine with a single, larger combustion chamber: for real-world testing of this engine, several test benches were built at the Peenemünde plant.
The engine was supposed to have a thrust of 200,000 kgf, and a diameter of 4.12 meters.

- A9: This was the second stage of the missile, which was also partially tested.
  In its initial configuration, it was to consist of a normal A4 with two small wings on the side. The experiments were carried out on the A4b, which was essentially a "production" V-2 with wings and increased weight. Two examples of this were launched, on 27 December 1944 and 24 January 1945.
  The first test was unsuccessful: the subsequent launches, although planned, were never carried out due to the disastrous course of the conflict.
  However, the final configuration of the A9 envisaged a sort of human-piloted rocket plane, characterised by two small lateral wings along the entire fuselage: this solution, in fact, according to tests conducted in the wind tunnel, would have brought about a whole series of advantages, both during supersonic flight and in terms of assembly with the first stage.

One of the major problems that had to be faced was the guidance system: the great range, in fact, made this weapon system extremely imprecise.
For this reason, the designers considered the use of human piloting. According to the planned mission profile, therefore, the

A9 should have separated from the first stage at an altitude of 390 km and at a speed of 3,400 m/s.

It was then supposed to begin a reentry phase, heading towards its target guided by radio or by submarines located in the Atlantic Ocean.

The pilot, once he had framed the target, should have blocked the aircraft's course and ejected.

The problem was that it was a very risky maneuver: not only

was it potentially deadly, but even if successful it would have led to the certain capture of the man piloting the missile.

The final A10 design stood about 20 metres (65 ft) tall. Powered by a 375,000 lbf (1,670 kN) thrust rocket, burning diesel fuel and nitric acid, its 50-second burn would have propelled its A9 second stage to a speed of about 4,300 km/h (2,700 mph) and an altitude of 394 km (245 mi).

A11

The A11 was a three-stage missile project capable of both launching a 500 kg artificial satellite into low Earth orbit and being used as an intercontinental ballistic missile.

Continued in 1944, it was the A10 to which a stage, the A11, was to be added, consisting of a cluster of six A10 engines.

Like the A10, the A11 was to be fitted with wings, so that it could be used for bombing missions or recovered later.

The height of this missile was supposed to reach 41.5 meters, with a diameter of 8.1 meters and a launch weight of 586,000 kg: the estimated apogee was 300 km.

The range, as previously mentioned, was supposed to reach 5,000 km.

A12

The A12 missile was a true orbital missile.
It was proposed as a four-stage, comprising A12, A11, A10 and A9.
Calculations showed that it could place up to 10 tons of payload into low Earth orbit.
The A12 would have weighed around 3,500 tonnes with full tanks and would have been 33 metres tall: it was to be powered by 50 A10 engines, fuelled by liquid oxygen and alcohol.

Launch Sites

On 18 December 1942 a military deployment plan was drawn up following Hitler's decision on 22 November that the V-2s were to be prepared and launched from fortified installations (bunkers).
The first works began at the end of March 1942 in the following locations:

- Eperlecques: northern France, Pas de Calais department.
- Wizernes: northern France, Pas de Calais department.
- Sottevast: northern France, Manche department, in the Lower Normandy region.
- Brecourt: The assault on Brécourt Manor was a clash between U.S. paratroopers of the 101st Airborne Division and German troops positioned south of Utah Beach, during the early stages of the Normandy landings, in the midst of the Second World War.
- Rinxent: northern France, Pas de Calais department.
- Caumont: northern France, Calvados department, in the Lower Normandy region.
- Dieppedalle: northern France, department of Seine-Maritime, in the Upper Normandy region.

Following numerous bombing operations, these sites were later abandoned, despite new construction techniques that significantly increased their protection, opting for mobile launch sites scattered around the region.
This new type of launch method had become established at the beginning of 1944 following numerous aerial bombardments.

In the departments of Nord and Pas de Calais, 23 launch sites for the V -2 were set up in forests and sometimes in the parks of certain castles, well protected from prying eyes.

Each launch site consisted of two to three launch pads: these constructions took the form of simple concrete platforms measuring 20 metres by 11 metres and were difficult to identify. Of the 6,500 V-2 units produced by German industry, 3,170 were launched on targets:

- 1,664 on Belgium (1,610 on Antwerp, 27 on Lüttich, 13 on Hasselt, 9 on Tournai, 3 on Mons, 2 on Dienst).
- 1,403 on England (1,359 on London, 43 on Norwich, 1 on Ipswich).
- 73 on France (25 on Lille, 19 on Paris, 19 on Tourcoing, 6 on Arras, 4 on Cambrai).
- 19 on the Netherlands (on Maastricht).
- 11 on Germany (target the Remagen bridge over the Rhine, taken intact by American troops in 1945).

The V-2s, in the post-war period, became the starting point for the construction of all the large families of ballistic missiles developed in the Soviet Union, Great Britain, France and the United States, where von Braun, despite his "controversial " past, became the father of the American space program.

V-2 and submarines

In order to launch the V-2s on American soil, it was planned to turn to the Kriegsmarine, but this was not so simple because, after all, the A-4/V-2 missile was an army program.

However, the Oberkommando wanted this solution and in December 1944 overcame all resistance from the German Armed Forces and on the 11th of that month set up the Study Committee in Peenemunde to carry out a very difficult project:

- Transporting and launching from the sea an A-4 missile, which was already difficult and dangerous to fire from land under standard conditions.

Dr. Dikmann from the Vulcan shipyard, Eng. Riedel, and Gen. Rosmann became interested in the project and the group was called Elektro Mechanishe Werke Karlshagen.

- At the end of the design, a submarine-shaped container weighing 500 tons and 45 meters long was achieved.

With cruciform control surfaces and a nose cone that opened into two sections when needed, it had the missile inside in the front part, underneath was the ethyl alcohol tank and underneath that, the liquid oxygen and hydrogen peroxide, including the trim pumps and ballast tanks.

- The whole thing was controlled by cable, the same one that made the container towed by the submarine.

For the launch, the system had to become vertical, with a maximum inclination of 1.5 degrees: the missile certainly could not be carried already loaded and ready for launch, it was already a step forward to have the warhead ready.

Once the container was ready, the personnel left the "floating ramp" with a dinghy, and then the missile, at the moment of launch, broke through the lateral bulkheads that were frangible due to the exhaust gases.

The container was not disposable: each U-boat, probably of the Type XXI or IX type, had to carry two of them in tow and pull for 300 km, but after launch the containers could be ballasted and towed back to base, or entrusted to supply submarines, thus making it possible to use the U-boat for "normal" tasks.

After that, the Vulkan shipyards in Stettin were quick to deliver the prototype and launch series production.

- The first and only launch was carried out after March 25, the day of delivery, in the Baltic Sea, near Peenemunde.

It was apparently a success, and plans were made to build 60 launchers that would have delivered 500 V-2s a month to the United States.

This would have required each launcher to be used at least twice a week, and 250-500 sorties a month to the US: considering the losses of German submarines, it is difficult that these results could have even been approached.

- After all, the firing campaign of the much simpler V-1s was planned at 3,000 weapons per day, when the maximum was 316.

It was all very ambitious.

In fact, the problems would have been enormous: navigating with one or two containers of this kind in the middle of the Atlantic, surfaced or submerged (the compensation boxes of these 'wire-guided submarines' also allowed for underwater movement) would have been an extremely difficult undertaking in itself, even without considering the technical problems of the V2s.

In stormy conditions it would have been difficult to obtain the conditions for an accurate launch, since even from the ground, knowing exactly where you were throwing from, the error was a few km.

At 300 km, and at sea, there was no way to know one's position with absolute precision: all this, then, did not consider that the United States in 1945 was quite dangerous for U-boats even when it came to operating in Europe.

A slow and tiring navigation towards New York would have had to take into account the efforts made by the USN. To stop for hours in front of the American coasts would have been extremely dangerous, the "easy" times of early 1942 were long gone.

The difference between this solution, even if technically acceptable, and what was later realized is indicative, just think of the Russian "Golf" and "Hotel" type submarines with missiles derived from the V-2. But these submarines had the missiles integrated inside them, in large and stable platforms.

- Perhaps for the V-2s, large submarines such as the Japanese I-401s would have been more than sufficient for the purpose.

Certainly, if one of these actions had succeeded, it would have been a propaganda coup of considerable importance for Germany. But in March 1945, the Americans were crossing the Rhine, and the Third Reich had only weeks to live, while fuel was running low for every branch of the armed forces.

If Germany had been able to launch a nuclear V-2, it might have had some impact on the fate of the nation: however, it is difficult to understand why the much simpler V-1s were not considered for launch from a large submarine.

This was basically done, in the post-war period, with an American program that involved the Loon, a copy of the V-1, which were then developed until reaching the powerful Regulus I and II missile (supersonic). Just think of the submarines with various seaplanes and the relative cumbersome arrangements.

However, V-1s do not appear to have ever been considered, perhaps because of their vulnerability, as under-launched weapons.

Operation Backfire

If the Americans had gotten their hands on the V-2 and other advanced technologies with the 'Paperclip' project, which began on July 19, 1945 with the hiring of numerous German technicians, the English, who suffered more than anyone else from the missile attacks, were quick to do the same, and moreover preceded the Americans, whose first launch of a V-2 at White Sands on April 16, 1946 was also a failure. Instead, the English, with considerable cunning, and also a good dose of luck, managed to launch 3 missiles from Cuxhaven: this despite the fact that on May 30, 14 tons of German documents were brought from Antwerp to the United States: they were the treasure found in a mine in Dornten, where, however, they remained for a very short time.

Along with these they took away roughly the equivalent of 400 railway wagons with enough to assemble about 100 V-2s. But with the Soviets and the Americans racing to grab what remained of the German technology and the technicians and scientists that were needed, the third competitor was able to enjoy it, at least for the time being.

The 21st Army Group recruited personnel from the Netherlands and West Germany to rebuild a V-2 rocket launch battery, and even before von Braun surrendered to the Americans on 2 May 1945, the British had begun, thanks to the idea of Commander J.C.Bernard.

Operation Backfire, so called according to Colonel Carter's idea, managed to find 30 vehicles to set up a real launch unit by May 20.

The British thought they would soon have thirty missiles, but they did not know that the V-2s were "perishable" materials that had to be launched within a week to avoid ending up with internal components that would fail due to even the slightest humidity or other problems caused by the environment.

- In fact, it would have been better to launch within three days to reduce the malfunctions to only 4% rather than 20%, as initially happened against Great Britain.

In the end it was decided that Cuxhaven was suitable for the experimental launch of these weapons, to be reduced in range to 240 km instead of 320 km to avoid the risk of hitting Denmark.
But on May 26, it was officially realized that the V-2s found were not in such conditions to ensure the planned firing campaign, much to the chagrin of the English who had this idea.
In fact, the era of missiles guaranteed for ten years without maintenance (or almost) and of ICBMs capable of remaining on alert even for consecutive years, was still far away.
The surviving factories were mostly moved to the East to protect them from Allied bombs, meaning that, despite the moves to the South towards the end of the war, they were now in Soviet hands.
For six weeks, a search was conducted for all the small firms that were subcontractors of the 30,000 components of the V-2, despite the fact that there were not even enough manuals and those that existed did not agree with each other, since the production batches of the V-2s were not necessarily compatible.
Despite all the difficulties, 400 trucks and 640 tons of tools, as well as the construction drawings, finally arrived.

- Despite all the difficulties, the Germans, to the amazement of the Allies, had carried out firings until March 1945, but now there was no way of having enough subsystems to assemble any V-2s.

Many components, such as the graphite blades for the jet deflectors, had been sabotaged, even the last V-2 at Peenemunde was blown up on its ramp on February 27, 1945, when von Braun set foot there for the last time.

In the end, however, there were 2,500 English and nearly 4,000 Germans in Cuxhaven, including people from von Braun's staff. Many things had to be procured, and the Germans had to be trusted, headed by Colonel Weber.

- A 90-meter-long workshop was built, and finally a plant was found for the production of liquid oxygen, of which 5 tons were needed to launch a V-2, but in reality 9 tons were needed to compensate for the losses.

It needed at least 93% pure alcohol, which came from Nordhausen, and so on. On October 2, 12 V-2s were discovered, 8 of which were in almost perfect condition.

Now all the 'pieces' were really assembled: with few resources, beating the Americans and the Soviets to the punch, the English moved on to the first post-war shootings.

An attempt was made to launch the V-2s as early as October 2, but nothing happened. But on October 3, at 2:43 p.m., the V-2 was actually launched.

It arched into the sky and in just 4 minutes and 50 seconds hit a point 2.4 km to the left and about 1.6 km short, still better than an artillery shell of equivalent range.

- Then came a V-2 on October 4, which, however, only travelled 24 km in 35 seconds, and, finally, on October 15, 1945 another missile was fired, this time with a large crowd of Allied guests, and, to the relief of the British, and despite a wind of 43 km/h, the launch worked perfectly.

The mission was over and, as of October 20, when the personnel were released, only twenty agreed to continue working with the British.

So, this kind of "circus" dissolved without further consequences, except for a 40-minute documentary, 5 volumes delivered in January 1947 to the Ministry of War, and various

materials placed in museums.
The English suffered no further consequences.
They paid much less than the Americans and the Soviets, and perhaps that also counted.
Despite this lack of German contribution, English rocketry also had a very interesting development, with original projects that were separate from what was being produced in the rest of the world. But it started late, also because, despite being the first to make a V-2 work after the war, they did not obtain lasting consequences for their technology: an extemporaneous and resounding success, which, however, in impoverished Great Britain they did not know how or did not want to realize.

V-2s in the Soviet Union

The Soviets entered Peenemunde on May 5, 1945, getting their hands on the "Holy Grail" of advanced research at the time.
But they did not find much of interest, when the centre, defended to the last by the SS, was by now stripped of many of its resources, such as the Wurzuburg Riese radar, the supersonic wind tunnel of Mach 4.4 built by Rudolph Hermman (sent to Bavaria, to Kochel).

- Furthermore, the test stands had almost all been damaged, including those for the Wasserfall missiles and the smaller Taifun-type SAMs.

The Bank 1 still present, was the one to which the 25 ton thrust rocket engine was connected in the spring, later brought to 27 even if 1.3 were "eaten" by the graphite directional panels.
It was not only the Soviet advance that led to the move towards the South of Germany, but also the fear of other raids, such as the one by the RAF on 17-18 August 1943, which was paid for dearly, destroying much of the infrastructure, killing 735 people, of whom over 600 were prisoners of war who had been reduced to forced labor.

- Dr. Thiel, the designer of the C-1 Wasserfall engine and the A-4 (the V-2), also died on this occasion.

Not only that, he was also the designer of a monstrous engine intended for an intercontinental ballistic missile called A-9 or A-1: in fact, the same bench 1 was capable of withstanding over 200 tons of thrust and this engine reached, at least in design, 180.
It was hard to put all the pieces back in place now.
For example, the V-2s were built based on 6,450 construction

drawings, had 30,000 various components, but many of the machines had been brought to the 111,000 m2 underground factory in Thuringia, 260 km away.

Test stands were also needed for the V-2 engines, which had to be shown to function correctly for at least 65 seconds, served by a system using something like 115 kg of liquid oxygen per minute.

But not much remained of all this, nor of the 4,325 technicians and 760 employees still present in February, much to the chagrin of Col. Vavilov who led the troops that reached Peenemunde.

The fact is that von Braun had decided to opt for moving towards the West and the Germans did not want to leave valuable materials and men in Peenemunde, starting the migration to Thuringia on February 17, 1945, with a train of 525 people.

- In short, the Soviets were initially left empty-handed: the Americans, on the other hand, found 250 V-2s at the Mittelwerk.

But it was an area assigned to the Soviet Union, so it should have been "theirs": instead, in nine days the Americans made 640 tons of materials disappear in 300 railway cars, including 510,101 drawings and 3,500 reports.

- On May 2, von Braun was in Bavaria with his best technicians and their families, ready to surrender to the Americans.

Ninety of them actually went to France and became the backbone of French rocketry up to the Ariane 4.

But all was not lost, because of the 2,000 V-2s available at the end of March 1945, about half were in German zones that were under Soviet control.

Thus, 515 V-2s were immediately sent to Russia, but there were so many reliability problems that they practically had to be rebuilt.

- This is not surprising, since the engines already had 500 subsystems and 1,800 elements, and above all the economy with which the V-2s were built was such that they had to be launched with a real deadline: within seven days of completion.

Due to damaged valves, gyroscopes and electrical resistors, up to 20 percent of the V-2s delivered to units had to be returned for "rework at Mittelwerk," or to be used as spare parts for new ones.

As if that were not enough, the captured V-2s were usually sabotaged, such as the gyroscopes and graphite jet deflectors: finally, rust was an additional problem during those months of storage.

The Soviets reached the underground base at Nordhausen only on July 5, only to find it again plundered by the Americans.

At least there was no shortage of production machinery, especially since the construction rate had reached 500 units per month in January, but there was almost no usable operational missile.

- Toakaev, one of the leading Russian rocket experts, was rather depressed even though he was thinking of organizing a working group in Germany to rebuild the V-2 with all the German technicians forced or still available volunteers.

Now the problem was that in the West there were already many "customers" of German technology: the last V-2 was fired on London no later than March 28, 1945, but in October three British V-2s were fired from Cuxhaven just to evaluate their ballistics.

In truth, there was little to evaluate given that in the 200 days of bombing on London 3,065 V-2s had rained down, with an error on the target of 2.5%, which however meant about 7 km at maximum range.
Above all, reliability had proven exceptional, with over 90% of launches successful, although the missiles often exploded on reentry into the atmosphere despite all attempts to insulate the warhead well.
It took a lot of hard work, however, for the Soviets and on October 18, 1947, over 2 years later, they finally launched a V-2 from Volgograd and, thanks only to the German "Collective of Specialists", volunteers or not.

- The improved version, the R-1, waited until 18 October 1948.

Among the protagonists of the birth of Soviet rocketry was also Colonel Valentin Glunsko Korolev, who survived the "Stalinist purges" that affected him, but was rehabilitated thanks to the KGB that appreciated his skills as a designer, and who spoke German well. This was a notable advantage, because he did not have to wait for the documents to be translated, while he could speak or question German scientists and technicians directly.
It wouldn't have been easy even then, with Stalin wanting the drawings restored and a production line set up in Germany.
So, under the not-so-veiled threat of ending up in a gulag, the three Soviets went to work establishing RABE in Berlin, under the command of General Kutsentsov.
Qualified people were needed for the V-2 cloning program, and among these the best was certainly Helmu Grottrup, an expert in electronics and guidance systems, who was paid 5,000 marks a month if he accepted the job, four times what von Braun was earning with the Americans.
And, in fact, there were concrete hopes that he might change sides, which would also change history.

But what the Soviets had hoped for did not happen.
This scientist was also very good at the "pyramidal" work structure tested at Peenemunde, with a final contact and many super-specialists to create the components: this was how von Braun presented himself to the Americans, with 118 technicians and the launch director Kurt Debus.
Grottrup quickly replaced the first, less than stellar director Dr. Rosemplenter at RABE and, through a series of hirings, expanded the staff from 30 to 5,000 people in just one year.

- Eventually, 30 new V-2s were shipped to Russia, and several centers were established for specialized tasks, such as Werk II for the V-2 engines.

Finally, a Soviet order came for an experimental train of 80-100 cars, to carry out experimental launches of the V-2, although officially it was only a "mobile meteorological train".
However, there will never be any more V-2 launches from Germany.
Tests continued in Lehesten, where Glushko had already produced a high-powered engine in September: then, in the summer of 1946, requests for technical improvements for a greater range began. The secrecy of the work was such that for years even the construction of the R-7 (SS-6) missile remained uncertain, so much so that even at the end of the 1950s it was thought that they were equipped with only 5 R-14 engines with 120 tons of thrust, engines that had never existed in this form.
Among the modifications made, there was the one to make the warhead detachable with explosive bolts to increase the range, a sort of two-stage missile: in reality, these were old ideas for missiles already tested towards the end of the war, equipped with such characteristics.

The fact is that on May 13, 1946, Stalin had created the State Commission for the Study of Long-Range Rockets or PKRDD. This had promptly established various OKBs, such as Glushko's OKB-456 MAP, for endoreactors, and various institutes such as Korolev's NII-88 MW for ballistic rockets, NII-885 MPSS for guidance systems, and others, including the Council of Designers, which grouped together the various branches of guidance, propulsion and launch systems.

- Korolev would then have all the experiences and progress of the other centers and OKBs flowed into his OKB, which in 1954 became OKB-1.

There were also the Zadov 88 and 456 factories, to which missiles and components produced at the Zentralwerke and its German subsidiaries were promptly shipped: in this way, the work of the 7,000 East German employees was "passed on" to the Soviets, to mislead the Americans as to the origin of such progress.

The first improved missiles were the R-1 with a slightly improved propulsion system, known as the SS-1 Scunner to NATO, and the R-2, which would have double the original range, known as the SS-2 Sibling.

It goes without saying that at this point, to make the most of missiles, which were in any case expensive and imprecise, it was necessary to have an atomic warhead: but this too was on its way.

Meanwhile, Stalin wanted to concentrate all the work in Soviet territory and on October 22, 2,500 Germans, including Grottrup, were ordered to leave Germany (he had accepted the Soviet contract precisely to avoid leaving it) and found themselves distributed in various locations and factories. In the end, however, they found themselves mostly grouped together in Gorodomljia.

Among their tasks were some bizarre ones, such as testing the

possibility of an "antipolar bomber," as hypothesized by Sanders, with a 100-ton thrust engine that had been partially realized during the war.
A sort of Space Shuttle ante litteram, which was supposed to go into orbit and then carry out bombing raids on enemy territory.
Thanks to them, improved versions of the A-4/V2 engines were also born:

- The RD-100, with more divergent exhausts to increase thrust output.
- The RD-101 with 40% higher pressure is used for R-2.
- The RD-103 with 60% increased exhaust pressure and used for the R-5 or SS-3 Shyster, 1,200 km, while the RD-102 was an intermediate stage that was never realized.

Other types of weapons were later studied, such as the 600 km range G-1, called R-4 or R-10 by the Soviets, which had self-supporting tanks (i.e. pressurized to 2 atmospheres, which made the missile structure lighter, albeit with an increase in thickness from 1.5 to 4 mm), so much so that the range was later extended to 810 km, while the guidance systems were moved under the tanks.
The head was covered in wood but made non-flammable with an appropriate chemical process: however, it remained on paper, but it was an interesting prototype.
In 1947, the first Soviet cosmodrome, called Volgograd Station, was formed, preceding Baikonur by about 8 years.
Much of the equipment was on the two German special trains, FMS-1 and 2, mentioned earlier.
Grottrup and other technicians were sent there and on 18 October at 10.47 am they were able to launch the missiles with a V-2 model T (telemetric) which was launched at over 206 km, although the second launch, two days later, saw the weapon stop at 152 metres and then fall back, prompting accusations of

sabotage.
Further tests followed and then the Germans set off again for Gorodomljia.
In 1948, work began on a 2,500 km range missile with a 1,000 kg warhead, which was called G-2 by the Germans and R-12 or R-6 by the Soviets.
There was a need for a new project with engines of 100 tons of thrust: the project was interesting, but it was surpassed by the G-4 for 3,000 km and 3 tons of thrust, requested on 9 April 1949 by Minister Ustinov.
The reason was the possibility of transporting the Soviet atomic bomb throughout Europe, and, in fact, on August 29 of that year the first "atomic bomb" was detonated.
So, this missile was studied but it did not have a long life either: it had a single stage 23.65 meters high with a base diameter of 2.74 meters, a weight of 70 tons when fully loaded and just 6,160 when empty, with an engine with 101 tons of thrust.

- It had a warhead protected by 400 kg of steel and (internally) wood, a 60 atmospheres pressure engine, without a gas generator but with turbines powered by combustion gas.

On September 21, 1949, the first R-2 with a 37-ton RD-101 engine was rolled out: the Soviets, in the meantime, had taken over the drawings and the material produced by the Germans, who finally hoped to do something more than consultants to increase the fame of local scientists, such as Korolev.
There were also other projects, such as the R-3 with a range of 4,000 km, and then, to be improved, such as the R-3A, ancestor of the intercontinental R-7: this was the work of Glunshko, with a 7,000 kgs engine and conical nozzles replaced by the more complex divergent ones, which gained about 3% of the thrust.
Other ideas were perhaps taken from the 8,000 kgs engines of the anti-aircraft Wasserfall.

Finally, 3,000 kg vernier rockets were conceived, which were an alternative to the much more complex gimballed nozzles.
Finally, the Germans were sent back to Germany from March 21, 1951 to November 30, 1953, after they had effectively helped create a class of Soviet technicians whom they had trained.

- Meanwhile, the R-5 was launched, a missile that was the ultimate evolution of the V-2 technology.

In the R-5M version, this 20.74-meter weapon reached 1,200 km and could strike with a small nuclear warhead, which made it quite fearsome for the West.
It was produced in small series in 1956, and was the counterpart, but with a much greater range, of the American Redstone, also derived from V-2 technology.

- Finally, the Soviet rockets "offspring" of the V-2 and their technicians were converted into geophysical devices or for high-altitude atmospheric reconnaissance launches.

These were devices built as early as 1949 and designated with V-1 as the basic acronym and various sub-versions, up to 18 metres high, with scientific equipment: the first one already reached 110 km on 24 May 1949.
In 1955, a V-1E lifted a load of 1.8 tons, including dogs, rabbits and mice, to 100 km: then it was the turn of the R-2s converted into V-2s (certainly not the original ones), always with side containers that had equipment to be dropped by parachute or with warheads equipped with special aerodynamic brakes.
One of them, on May 16, 1957, reached 200 km with filming systems and chemical analysis equipment.

Dogs were launched en masse: at least 100 pairs in 1955-60 and the R-5 missile used from 1957, carried its load of 1,350 kg and two dogs to a height of 480 km.

He was taller than the others, a good 23.74 meters.

- In short, the Soviets built their first generation of ballistic missiles thanks to the efforts and contributions of the various Peenemundians, but they never gave them any credit, which did not fail to anger German scientists.

In 1958 Grottrup thus submitted to the German DGRR (a space flight society) a memoir that recounted the work he had been doing for years in the Soviet Union, at least to re-establish the historical truth.

The V-2 and the Birth of French Rocketry

It was France that had the dubious honor of being hit by the first A-4 ballistic missiles ever launched in war.

- This was Operation Penguin, which had Hans Krammler as its commander.

There were three battalions with as many as 6,300 soldiers and 1,600 vehicles, with the 485th Battalion in the North, and the 836th and 444th SS in the South.
The objective was essentially London, but Paris was also added, which was liberated at the end of August.
An attempt was made to launch two V-2s on September 6, but they failed due to defects in the ignition or fuel systems, but on September 8, at 8.34, after 4 minutes of flight, a missile from the 444th was successful, albeit launched from 290 km.

- Paris, however, was not particularly hard hit, as it had at most 22 V-2 launches, which missed their target by up to 70 km.

Perhaps there was no will to hit it, which was certainly not lacking for London and Antwerp, hit at the same time by 350 devices, starting on the same day with a shot near Waterloo Station, due to the activity of the 485th Battalion.
Initially, the English pretended that these were gas leaks, but then they had to admit that there were undetectable weapons reaching their capital: Henry Moureu, director of the State Research Laboratory in Paris, soon understood that these weapons were the future and France could not remain outside of them.
The Ministry of Aviation thought the same way and on 9 May 1945 gave him the mandate to recover everything possible,

together with the technician JJ Barré, who had tested the EA 1941, the first French liquid-propellant endoreactor, of about 1,000 kgs, on 17 March of that year.

- They wanted to obtain at least the V-1s and about ten V-2s: the former were granted by the Anglo-Americans, so much so that Nord Aviation used them as the basis for the CT-10 target aircraft, which was basically a clone of them with an Arsenal pulse jet.

But things went less well for the V-2s, and the only thing that resembled a claim to have V-2s was rummaging around Cuxhaven, where the British had very quickly begun testing, albeit unsuccessfully, the V-2s.

But there were certainly not many usable materials and the French had to make do with the little they managed to scrape together, especially with the help of DEFA (Directorate of Studies and Armaments Production), which among other things would soon give shape to the eponymous 30 mm DEFA cannon, derived from German revolver cannon technology.

On November 4, 1945, CEPA, the Center for the Study of Self-Propelled Weapons, was born.

- Its tasks were two: to rebuild the advanced German weapons, and to improve their range and war load: the technicians were found in Cuxhaven and Trauen for a total of 90 hired by 15 May 1946.

On May 17, a proposal was made to build a center that later became the headquarters of SEP, the manufacturer of the Ariane, in Vernon, a town in Normandy.

The German technicians were initially used divided into two groups, to study the guidance systems and the engine systems, but there was also a small detachment to build 1,000 hp tank engines, these being technicians from Maybach.

Among the innovations studied, there was a gas generator

patented already in 1942 by the engineer Bringer, who at the time worked with Thiel: it was a system in which the propellants burned at 3,000 degrees in a combustion chamber, a temperature that was then reduced to 600 degrees with distilled water, which served to pressurize, with the gases produced, the tanks, eliminating the large and heavy turbopumps.

- This alone was enough to increase the range of a V-2 to 550 km, but an engine with 40 tons of thrust was also wanted.

Meanwhile, the gas generator of this type, in many variations, will be used up to the Ariane 4 rockets: then the French, while trying to rebuild the V-2 in the workshops of Poteaux, thought of various new projects such as a 100 km ballistic missile, the radio-guided PARCA SAM missile, a sounding rocket and a strategic rocket called Eole.
Meanwhile, the V-2s assembled in the Poteaux workshops, despite all efforts, refused to materialize: only one of the thirty planned was completed in late 1947 and it was thought that the planned total would not be reached before 1952.
A missile that was over ten years old, however, did not represent the future, and so the planned A9 project with a nitric acid and diesel engine was thought of, combined with the entirely French EA 1946 project by engineer Barré, which, however, failed in two launches in 1952 and ended miserably.

- Even the Super V-2 or A9 did not fare better, being abandoned.

But engineer Bringer was told to continue developing the gas generator.

He also took an interest in small nitric acid and kerosene-powered rocket engines, a legacy of the Wasserfall engine.
In any case, in 1948, the Super V-2 project was cancelled, but in

compensation the German technicians at Vernon began to produce sounding rockets with excellent characteristics, up to systems for launching satellites.

- The first was the Veronique, similar to a small V-2, costing only $10,000, 6.5 meters long, 55 cm in diameter, with 710 kg of nitric acid and diesel fuel, 4,000 kgs engine for 31.5 seconds, total weight up to 1,435 kg.

It had no gyroscopes, but to stabilize itself it used 4 balanced tension cables on 4 horizontal rods, set to detach at 60 meters altitude, a regeneratively cooled engine, and variable altitude.

- Depending on the version, it went from 70 km to a good 200.

It entered production in 1952 and no fewer than 66 were launched until 1968, the last to inaugurate the Kaurou space base in French Guiana.

Years passed, and an attempt was made to launch a European program for the Europa launchers, but its subsystems were useful and Bringer first improved the Veronique and then devoted himself to the large Vesta, with a thrust of 14,400 kg, a weight of 5,400 kg and the ability to place a good 500 kg of load at an altitude of 600 km.

- Meanwhile, at ONERA in Chatillon, the French had succeeded in developing the LEX sounding rocket which weighed just 76 kg but was launched with an initial thrust of around 1,000 kg, which then dropped to around 200 kg in the following 30-35 seconds.

But after 8 successful launches it was abandoned despite having an interesting engine with carbon and nitro methane, i.e. a solid-liquid system.

In 1962, satellite launchers also arrived in Europe.

Space launchers based on the English Blue Streak ballistic

missile were wanted, but at the same time on 18 December 1961 the plan for the Diamant launcher was launched and the CNES, the Space Studies Centre, was established.
The Europa launchers, despite the London agreement of 23 March 1962 signed by seven nations, had no follow-up, but gave rise to the experience, later very useful, to the future space agency ESA.
Meanwhile, in France, technicians had assembled the 30-ton Verix engine system, used for the Emeraude rocket, but above all in November 1965 the Diamant A was launched, 18.9 metres high with two stages, consisting of an Emeraude and a Topaze.

- Finally, there was a small Rubis with a 41 kg payload carrying the Asterix satellite, which however stopped sending signals after a short time.

Other satellites will follow, Diapason on February 17, 1966 and Diadema on February 8, 1967.
These were launches carried out from Algeria, from the Hammaguir range, but this was later closed and all launches continued in Kourou, starting with two satellites DIAL and People, on the 23.5-metre Diamant B rocket with a payload of 160 kg.
The rocket was used until 1973, gradually improved, including the 40-ton thrust Valois engine, which was really the last of the possible evolutionary stages of Bringer's A9 project, and which thus carried a load of 200 kg to low orbits of 300 km, while the launch mass was 27.5 tons.
Only three launches, all by 1975.

- Finally came the Viking rockets for the Ariane.

It was Bringer again, with the last ten Germans from Vernon and many Frenchmen who were now well-educated in the sector, who tested on the test bench the 55-ton Viking 1 engine that was intended for the Europa 3 rocket, which would have been none other than the Ariane.

- It is incredible, but this engine was conceptually based on a functional 1,000 kgs type from 1942, a small prototype.

The engine cooling system was simplified with a water pump serving to cool the gases and the engine generator used the same main propellants.
It was much simpler than the equally powerful American Rocketdyne S.3 with a regenerative cooling system and a more complex structure in general.

- The 1971 Viking I was followed by the 73.5 ton Viking II.

In the end, the Ariane rockets were a complete success and the Viking engine was replaced only by the Vulcain with liquid hydrogen and oxygen.

- Eng. Karl-Heinz Bringer retired in 1976, after about 30 years of service with the Vernon Experimental Center, and died on January 2, 1999 at the age of 90.

One of the last of the 500 technicians from Peenemunde, who for decades had a major design and conceptual influence throughout the aerospace world.
People capable of designing systems in 1942 that were still valid 50 years later (one could also talk about Soviet developments such as the Scud missiles, for example), and who in all respects continued to do so, despite the dark shadow of the A4/V-2 program, which von Braun considered essentially a "necessary evil" to continue the space program on their career.
Like von Braun himself, who gradually fell into oblivion after his progressive disinterest in space missions, the others have tried in their professional lives to progress in the use of space propulsion, hoping perhaps one day to see the most important mission conceived by their leader realized: a manned space

mission to Mars , already foreseen in 1952 by von Braun.

They could certainly be defined as idealists in their drive towards this research, even if they were often manipulated by the military and politicians of the moment.

The Wasserfall

The Wasserfall was a large German anti-aircraft missile of the Second World War, but, like others of its class, it did not enter service in time.

- It was a massive weapon, similar to the SA-2, with a calculated range of as much as 48 km.

Its designs served as models for the American Hermes-A1 missile and for the Soviet research program known as R-101.

- The Wasserfall was essentially an anti-aircraft development of the V-2 missile, retaining the same shape and design, although equipped with additional fins placed halfway down the fuselage to increase maneuverability.

Work on the future Wasserfall project began in 1941 at the initiative of Walter Dornberger, one of the leaders of the rocket research center at the Peenemünde test site.
The idea was to create a liquid-fueled missile with radio control, capable of hitting enemy bombers in formation.
Preliminary study of the project continued until the autumn of 1942, when the technical requirements for the new air defense system were published.
It is worth noting that on September 25, 1942 Goering had authorized the development of four types of surface-to-air missiles:

- Unguided missiles (Taifun).
- Target-seeking guided missiles (Enzian).
- Optically guided missiles (Rheintochter and Schmetterling).
- Radar-guided missiles (Wasserfall).

Based on these ideas, the Wasserfall missile itself and auxiliary units were developed, while in the spring of 1943 the first laboratory tests began.
Within the framework of the Waterfall project, three variants of the rocket were developed with the designations:

- Wasserfall W-1: In the first version of the Wasserfall, the wings were longer and less raked than in later versions. In addition, the four wings located in the central part of the rocket body were offset by 45° from the tail fins.
  This was thought to help prevent aerodynamic screening of the turning mechanisms by the tailfin wings, but subsequent wind tunnel tests showed that this was not necessary.

- Wasserfall W-5: In the second design, the W-5 was slightly larger and the wings were smaller and swept back. The W-5 was credited with a maximum speed of 2,736 km/h, a ceiling of 18,300 meters (60,000 ft) and a range of about 26 km. German sources estimate the unit production cost of the Wasserfall at between 7,000 and 10,000 marks, requiring 1/8 of the man-hours required to produce the strategically ineffective A-4/V-2 missile.

- Wasserfall W-10: The final version, the W-10, was similar to the W-5, except that it was 27% smaller, to help save materials. The Wasserfall W-10 weighed 3,500 kg, had a diameter of 0.72 m, a wingspan of 1.58 m, and a length of 6.12 m.

During the initial launch phase, direction was controlled by four graphite rudders located in the rocket's exhaust stream, similar to the V-2 system: at higher air speeds, control passed to four air rudders mounted on the rocket's tail.
Since it was intended to reach only the flight altitude of the

large Allied bombers, it was reduced to about a quarter of its size compared to the V-2: 7.85 metres long, it weighed 3,700 kg, had a range of 25 km and a maximum speed of 770 metres per second (2,772 km/h).
Unlike their ancestors, the Wasserfalls were designed for launches that could be spread out over periods of a month or more, so liquid oxygen, which was too volatile, was not suitable for the purpose.

- Accordingly, a new engine was designed, by engineer Walter Thiel, which used a hyperbolic (self-igniting) fuel mixture of Visol, vinyl isobutyl ether, and RFNA, composed of 94% nitric acid and 6% dinitrogen tetroxide.

This hypergolic propellant was pushed into the combustion chamber together with nitrogen released from a separate tank.

- Originally, the warhead was 100 kg but was later replaced with a 306 kg one based on a liquid explosive.

The idea was to create a large explosive effect in the centre of the enemy bomber formation, which could theoretically bring down several aircraft with a single missile fired, with an operator detonating the warhead by remote control.

- The original intent was to install Wasserfall anti-aircraft batteries to defend all German cities with a population greater than 100,000, which would have resulted in approximately 200 Wasserfall batteries, deployed in three lines approximately 80 km apart.

Furthermore, with up to 300 missile batteries, it was possible to defend all of Germany from enemy bomber attacks.
For this grandiose plan, 5,000 missiles would be needed per month and it was estimated that each missile would require 500 hours of work: for comparison, each V-2 missile required 4,000 hours of work.

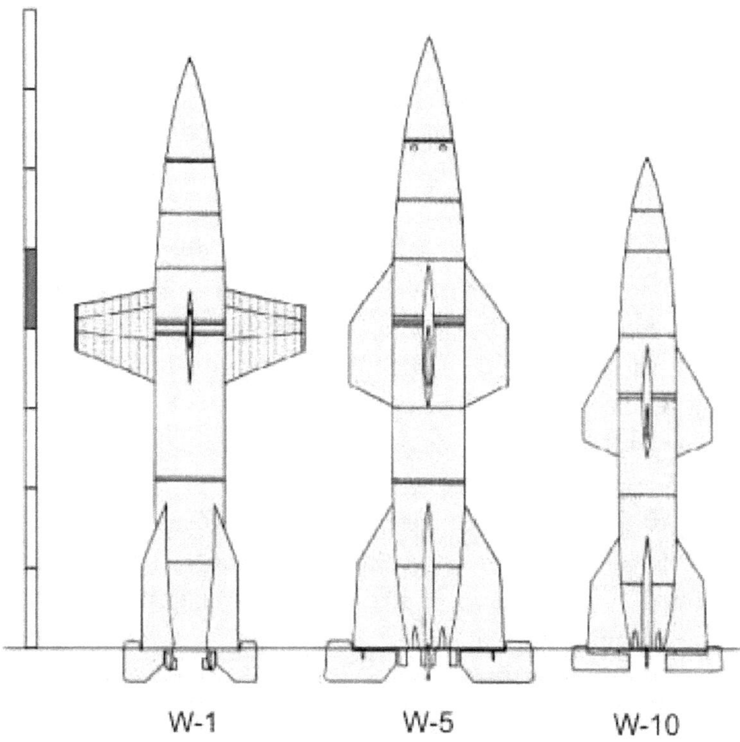

- The first Wasserfall site could have been set up as early as November 1945, with a total of 20 more sites set up within another four months with 100 Wasserfalls available for each site.

It was further estimated that production figures would reach 900 missiles per month by March 1946.
The missile used an automatic gyro for pitch/roll/yaw control, with pitch, roll and yaw control forces generated by mechanically coupled tail surfaces and graphite thrust vectoring vanes in the exhaust.

The guidance system was based on a MCLOS type radio

control, against daytime targets, while, for night launches, the use of this rocket was much more complex given the poor visibility of both the rocket itself and the target.

- With the MCLOS system, the operator had to keep an eye on both the missile and the target simultaneously and guide the missile to the target.

Typically, the missile was operated with a joystick, which used a modified version of the FuG 203/FuG 230 "Kehl-Straßburg" (codename Burgund) radio guidance system.
This technology, originally developed to guide anti-ship missiles from bombers, had previously been employed in controlling both the engine-less Fritz X and the rocket-powered Henschel Hs 293.
For the anti-aircraft role, the control mechanism was installed next to a chair, on a structure that allowed the operator to recline and easily observe targets overhead, rotating if necessary to maintain visual contact with the target.

- The MCLOS required considerable training and practice to master, so the accuracy achieved by MCLOS missiles is difficult to depict, as it was highly dependent on the skill of the operator.

To overcome this problem , two other advanced radar guidance schemes were under development.

- The first was the Rheinland, which was a manually operated line-of-sight system, using a transponder beacon in the missile and a tracking radar, for both the missile and the target, allowing night attacks on RAF bombers or daytime attacks through an overcast sky.
- The second was a beam-guided automatic guidance system, which used two orthogonal fan-shaped beams, which rotated as the beam followed the target. In this system, the missile would automatically guide the beam

until impact.

Interestingly, the rotating reticle infrared seeker, developed by von Braun for the A4/V-2, never found its way into the Wasserfall program.

A total of 35 test launches of the Wasserfall missile were carried out before the evacuation of the Peenemünde site on 17 February 1945.

In a related event, the Bäckebo rocket, which was essentially a V-2 missile equipped with Wasserfall radio guidance, crashed in Sweden on 13 June 1944: this incident highlighted the ongoing experimentation and cross-application of technologies within the German rocket program during this period.

- All materials from the Waterfall project in the spring of 1945 went to the winners.

Soviet and American specialists carefully studied this development and even conducted their own tests, using both captured rockets and products already assembled independently according to German documentation.

- All this made it possible to determine the real possibilities and potential of the German rocket.

Based on the study results, only solutions in the engine and power system sector received high scores.

- Unlike other liquid-fueled rockets of the time, the Wasserfall could, in fact, remain fueled for a certain period of time without any risk.

"Wasserfall" missile on display at the National Museum of the U.S. Air Force.

A range of up to 25 km and an altitude of 18 km allowed it to fight against any aircraft of the time: in this sense, the Wasserfall project was ahead of all other developments of the time.

- It is worth noting that after the end of World War II, the R-101 missile was produced in the USSR on the basis of the Wasserfall missile and the A-1 Hermes missile in the USA.

However:

- The R-101, a post-war Russian version of the German Wasserfall surface-to-air missile, never went into production, but the technology was used for further development of surface-to-air and surface-to-surface missiles in Russia.
- The R-108 was the second-generation, all-Russian version of the R-101, itself derived from the German

Wasserfall. Development began in May 1949, but the missile did not reach the flight-test stage before its cancellation in 1951.

- The R-109, also a Russian derivative of the German Wasserfall, was an intermediate design between the R-101 and the R-108. The missile did not, however, reach the flight test stage, before being cancelled in 1951.

In addition to the Wasserfall, other surface-to-air missiles had also been developed, with varying degrees of success:

- The Rheintochter, a multi-stage solid-fuel air defense missile, 6.3 meters high with a diameter of 54 cm and a maximum payload of 150 kg of high explosive.
- The Schmetterling, a surface-to-air missile, was initially equipped with a BMW 109-558 liquid-fueled rocket engine, which later received a Walther HWK 1090-729. The latter used nitric acid and kerosene, plus alcohol for a first boost. To increase thrust, two Schmading 109-553 powder rockets were added.
- The Feuerlilie, which was designed in two configurations, the F25 and the F55, the number of which was the fuselage diameter in centimetres.
- The Enzian, a liquid-fueled missile, with 4 solid-fuel rockets for take-off, which reached Mach 0.66. The Enzian was guided by radar illumination and an infrared system and carried a 450 kg high-explosive warhead. The purpose of this missile was, essentially, to break up bomber formations to allow fighters and FlaK (anti-aircraft artillery) to destroy enemy bombers without them being able to protect each other.

www.ingramcontent.com/pod-product-compliance
Lightning Source LLC
LaVergne TN
LVHW010116170826
845678LV00012B/2435

* 9 7 8 2 3 7 2 9 7 3 3 6 6 *